but sometimes a splat

is much more than that!

The thing about splats is there's so many kinds.

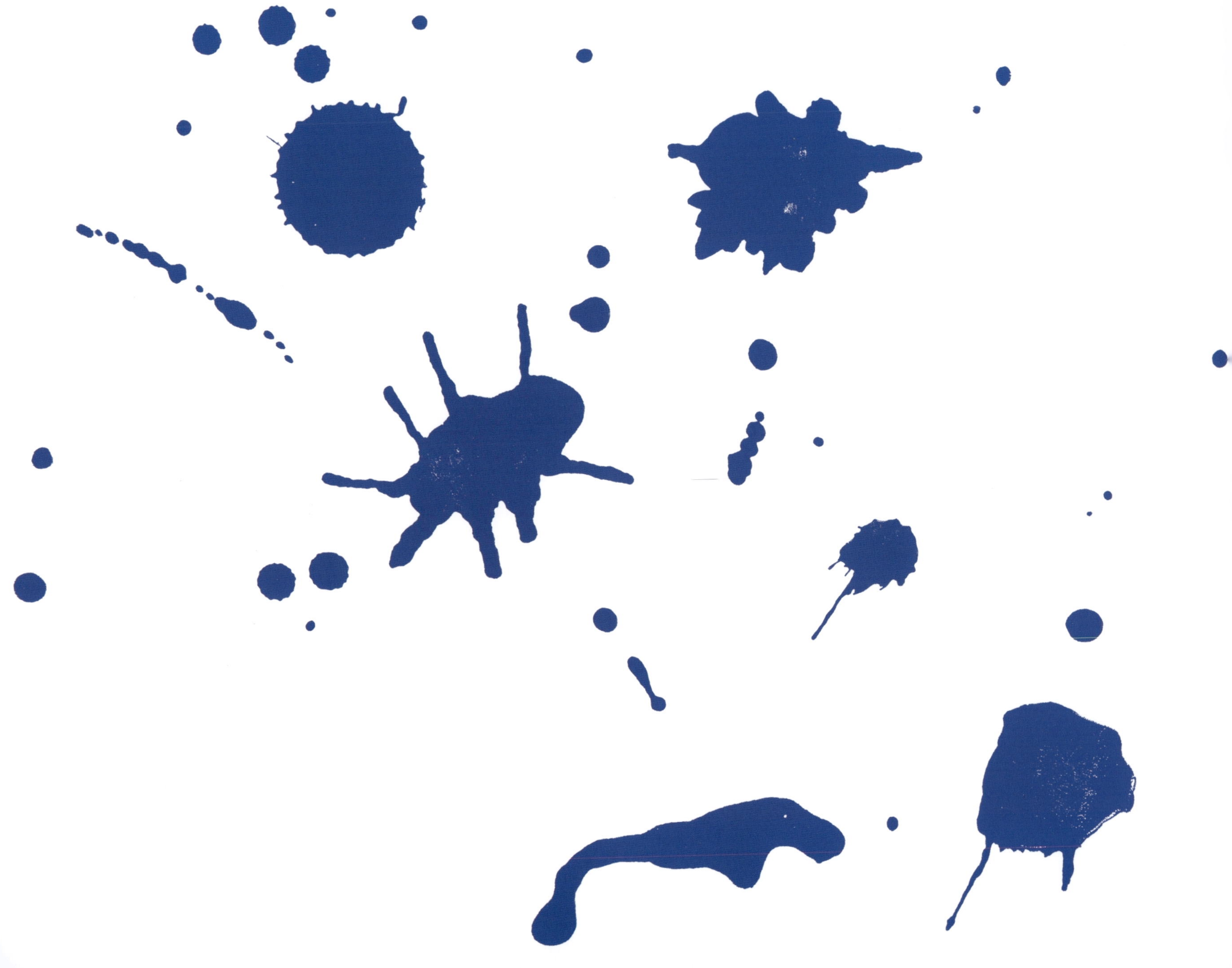

The more you look,
the more you
find.

Splats can be little

and splats can be BIG.

Some splats zag

and some splats zig.

There are splats that are empty

and splats that are full.

Some splats have feathers

and others have wool.

But wait a minute, what's *that* splat?

Is it this?

Or is it that?

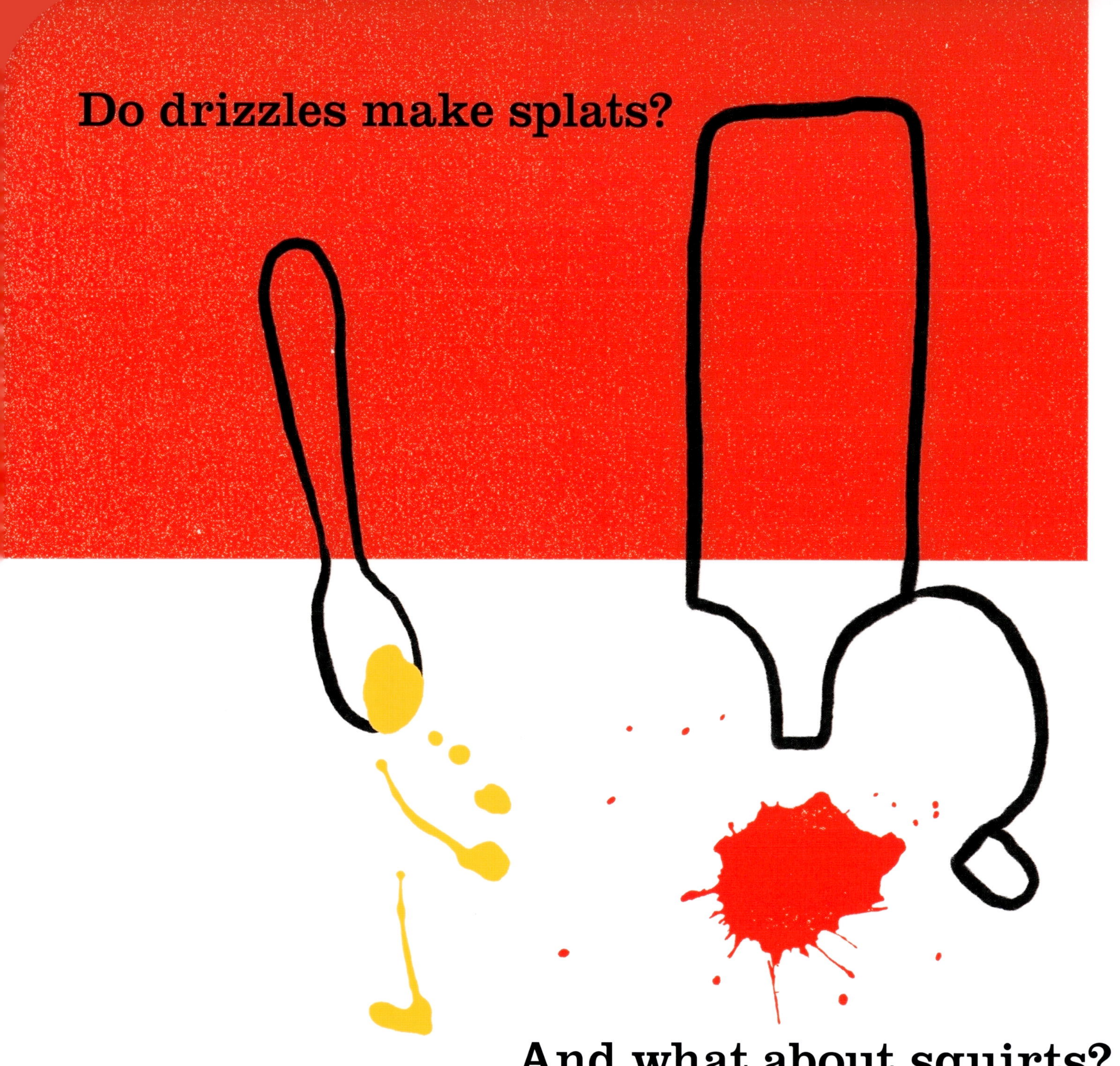

Do drizzles make splats?

And what about squirts?

Can splats be sour and also desserts?

There are splats that are red

and splats that are brown.

Splats that go up

and splats that come down.

Sometimes splats ROAR
and sometimes splats squeak.

Some splats cartwheel and some splats sleep.

And now, what will
this next splat be?

It's up to you.

What can you see?